NP JUMPSTART

MARKETING MADE EASY
FOR NURSE PRACTITIONERS

Krish Chopra, CEO/Co-Founder of NPHub &
Namar Al-Ganas, MHA

Copyright © 2020 Krish Chopra, CEO/Co-Founder of NPHub & Namar Al-Ganas, MHA.

All rights reserved. No part of this book may be reproduced, stored, or transmitted by any means—whether auditory, graphic, mechanical, or electronic—without written permission of the author, except in the case of brief excerpts used in critical articles and reviews. Unauthorized reproduction of any part of this work is illegal and is punishable by law.

ISBN: 978-1-7169-1907-7 (sc)
ISBN: 978-1-7169-1905-3 (e)

Because of the dynamic nature of the Internet, any web addresses or links contained in this book may have changed since publication and may no longer be valid. The views expressed in this work are solely those of the author and do not necessarily reflect the views of the publisher, and the publisher hereby disclaims any responsibility for them.

Any people depicted in stock imagery provided by Getty Images are models, and such images are being used for illustrative purposes only.
Certain stock imagery © Getty Images.

Lulu Publishing Services rev. date: 07/03/2020

PRAISE FOR NP JUMPSTART:

Krish is an essential part of any business. His marketing strategies are fresh and new, yet effective.

He's passionate about helping nurses and other healthcare professionals start, launch, and grow profitable businesses.

He has his pulse on relevant trends and an eye for businesses that are scalable.

*If you're looking to launch or grow your business, from inside-out, **Krish** is the way to go!*

- Portia Wofford
PW Enterprises

*I have thoroughly enjoyed working with **Krish**. He's a wonderful entrepreneur and cares greatly about helping others in the nursing profession. He is a thoughtful leader and will work tirelessly to help others reach their goals.*

-Dr. Heather Quaile DNP, WHNP-BC, SANE
CEO/Founder/Clinical Director Qubed Health Services LLC

*Working with **Namar** on my USP was a great experience. Starting my coaching business, I was overwhelmed with so many options, and I needed to understand what made one product or brand different than another. However, I didn't know the right way to position myself and my product in order to stand out. **Namar** helped me identify a unique selling proposition that allowed me to brand myself with my marketing decisions. He was prompt to my needs and applied great* listening skills to my requirements. His intake questions were well on target which allowed him to understand my needs in specific ways. He helped me create a plan to calculate the number of calls needed in order to hit my revenue goals. I strongly recommend **Namar** to anyone who wants to clarify their message and stand out among their competitors.

**-Johnny Dorvilien,
Owner True Life Purpose LLC**

Working with **Krish** was particularly helpful. I wanted to take care of patients- not focus on the business. He helped me realize I needed to do both and to prioritize what I was going to focus on and then seek help from my team for the things that weren't my strengths. He also helped me realize I was the face of the business and that my marketing plan needed to focus on that. From beginning to end he was helpful, supportive, and positive- exactly what I wanted and needed. I cannot recommend this book and him enough!

**-Melissa Hallman
DNP Founder, NP2ME**

CONTENTS

PRAISE FOR NP JUMPSTART: v

MISSION OF THIS BOOK xiii

PREFACE xv
    Why This Book? xvi
    Why Advanced Practice Providers? xviii
    Who is the NP Jumpstart Co-Author? xviii
    What is the Goal of NP Jumpstart? xix

CHAPTER 1: MARKETING MADE EASY 1
    The Jumpstart Checklist 4
    A Successful Marketing Strategy 5
    Patience is Key 6

CHAPTER 2: HOW TO GROW YOUR PRACTICE
WITHOUT SPENDING MONEY ON ADVERTISING 7
    Overview of the 5-Step Lean Marketing System 9

CHAPTER 3: THE FORMULA FOR UNLIMITED
REVENUE GROWTH 14
    Three Essential Avenues for Revenue Growth 17

CHAPTER 4: THE DIFFERENCE BETWEEN HIGH
PERFORMING CLINICS AND MEDIOCRE ONES 21
    Advantage #1: Create an Outstanding Patient Experience 22
    Advantage #2: Maximize Every Source of Revenue from
    the Clinic 23
    Advantage #3: Marketing Automation Saves Time 25

CHAPTER 5: STEP-BY-STEP MARKETING
AUTOMATION 27
    Example of Marketing Automation 28
    Are Marketing Automations Common in Private Practices?... 31
    Next Steps 32
    A Note to Remember 35
    Emailing Patients with an Offer: The Devil is in the Details .. 35

CHAPTER 6: MASTERING THE PATIENT
RELATIONSHIP 40
    Increase Repeat Business with Excellent Service:
    Top 5 Ways to "Wow" Your Patients 41

CHAPTER 7: HOW TO CREATE CONTENT EASILY 45
    Common Reasons Providers Don't Produce Videos 47
    The Krish Chopra Hack to Creating Content 48

CHAPTER 8: THE INCREDIBLE BENEFITS OF
OUTSOURCING 53
    How Outsourcing Can Help 54

CHAPTER 9: SIMPLE SEARCH ENGINE
OPTIMIZATION (SEO) PRACTICES TO RANK
HIGHER ON GOOGLE 56
    Best Practices to be Found Through SEO 57
    Video → Blog Transcription 57
    Content Collaboration 59
    Keyword Rankings on Search Engines 60

CHAPTER 10: MARKETING TO MILLENNIAL PATIENTS 61
The Importance of Social Media 62
Online Reviews 65
A Well-Performing Website 66
Conclusion on Millennials 70

CHAPTER 11: NOW, TAKE ACTION 71
Take Action 72
What to do Next 72

CHAPTER 12: WHY EVERY PRACTICE SHOULD CONSIDER PRECEPTING 75
What is a Preceptor and Precepting? 76
What Are the Benefits of Precepting? 77
A Common Objection to Precepting is Time Constraints 78

ABOUT THE AUTHORS 79

"This book is for the entrepreneur inside each and every Nurse Practitioner. Primary care needs YOU more than ever."

MISSION OF THIS BOOK

The goal of this book is to simplify marketing strategies for nurse practitioners who want to open or grow their private practice.

Any advanced practice provider (APP) who has a home health, Telehealth, clinic, online brand will learn the specific marketing strategies and tactics to grow their revenue and create a thriving practice.

PREFACE
Written by Krish Chopra

Dear Entrepreneurial Advanced Practice Providers,

Congratulations on taking the massive first step of purchasing this book.

Inside the next hundred pages or so, you're going to find the most complete and actionable marketing content you can use today to jumpstart your private practice!

Whether you've been in business for ten years or just starting out, these tactics will help you increase your patient base, bring back repeat patients, and create simple systems to free up your time!

The overwhelming support and demand for this book has been humbling! Across the country, providers are looking for new strategies to develop a strong practice and own their work-life balance as well as their financial future. The growing levels of entrepreneurship in healthcare inspires us every single day!

My name is Krish Chopra, and I am the co-founder and CEO of NPHub, a placement agency and marketplace dedicated to ending the preceptor shortage. Since 2013, I've been working with all types of advanced practice providers (nurse practitioners, certified nurse midwives, certified nurse anesthetists, clinical nurse specialists), as well as with medical doctors (MD), osteopathic physicians (DO), and physician assistants (PA).

Additionally, in 2019, I launched the popular interview series "5 Strategies to Grow Your Private Practice," interviewing over thirty private practice entrepreneurs! As a result, I've had a chance to work with, partner with, interview, or coach over 1,000 advanced practice providers, physicians, and practice managers over the past five years.

When working with newly owned practices and practice owners, I began noticing the same questions arise. And these questions often centered around marketing.

It was overwhelming! And when I realized the pattern, I began looking for an easy resource to share whenever I encountered the questions.

There weren't any.

This book will help Nurse Practitioners answer questions like:

- *How can I attract more patients?*
- *Is social media worth it? I post, but nothing happens!*
- *Am I using the right hashtags on social media?*
- *How do I increase that traffic with Google?*
- *Why does having more keywords help my website?*
- *Are videos better than anything?*
- *Should I upload to YouTube more often, do more live videos (like stories), or both?*
- *Does blogging do anything?*
- *How do I start without a big budget?*

Why This Book?

There needs to be a guide that outlines an easy-to-follow marketing strategy that an APP can implement within ninety days. In this book, we outline the exact strategies businesses inside and outside of healthcare are implementing to scale their revenue.

At its core, a medical practice is a service-based business, which means the tried and true marketing strategies work.

This book will require one thing from you, the reader. For the next 100 pages or so, let's pause our brain from focusing on patient care and patient outcomes.

Rather, let's shift our focus to the ***Patient Experience***.

What's the difference?

Patient care occurs when the patient is in the clinic, face-to-face with their provider. Patient experience is the holistic interaction the patient has with the organization, or in this case, your clinic.

One of the recurring messages I heard from my interview series in Authority Magazine and Thrive Global, "Strategies to Grow Your Private Practice," was that every successful private practice owner cited in some fashion that the role of the provider and the role of the business owner are completely different. If you want your practice to survive, you must wear both hats simultaneously.

Our hypothesis: the private practices that are failing are still thinking in an old-school mindset, where patients will come by walk-ins, referral networks, and word-of-mouth only. These methods still work, but these outdated marketing techniques alone are just not enough to thrive anymore.

We need to embrace the marketing tactics that are working right now, especially in the digital era with the widespread use of email and social media. The strategies outlined in this book are what hyper-successful practice owners are using to scale their business while they enjoy more free time.

Some of the strategies & tactics in this book may seem more difficult to implement than others. Some may seem easy in theory, but difficult to actually implement. Some strategies will cost money to implement, while some may require more time. Our recommendation is to focus on the achievable strategies that work for you.

If you follow the strategies outlined in the following pages, you will get tremendous value. Action is critical. It's better to implement one to two strategies outlined in this book than to dream about implementing ten different ones. Starting small is perfectly okay. Just start.

Why Advanced Practice Providers?

My thesis is simple: **Advanced practice providers are the future of primary care in the United States.** In my experience, there has been an explosion of entrepreneurship, especially in states where APPs have independent practice authority.

And yet, a practical guide doesn't exist.

Why is that?

I believe it's because advanced practice providers are underserved. They lack resources. For example, in a hospital setting, they often lack support from hospital administration/leadership teams, in the educational setting, they lack the resources to secure preceptors, and in the practice setting, they face numerous issues when dealing with insurance companies, including lower reimbursement rates. And in the entrepreneurial setting, they lack the marketing resources that are geared directly to them, the APP. Currently, everything in the market has been created for medical doctors, who have a different experience when first starting out on their own venture.

The healthcare market is still learning about APPs and the tremendous value they can provide patients and an ailing healthcare system. MDs are generally understood by the public and served with plenty of resources, such as business books and consulting services to help drive high performance. However, APPs aren't receiving the same level of support, and we aim to change that.

Who is the NP Jumpstart Co-Author?

I've partnered with Namar Al-Ganas to help bring as much value as possible to the readers of this book. Namar is a healthcare marketing and financial performance leader who has dedicated his career to helping healthcare providers and hospitals dramatically improve their business operations.

Namar and I have consulted and partnered with some of the brightest private practices in the United States and retooled the exact strategies

I've used to grow two successful businesses within four years for one purpose: to give a clear blueprint to jumpstart your private practice!

What is the Goal of NP Jumpstart?

Our goal when we first set out to create this book was simple: **to create a guide for advanced practice providers that delivers marketing strategy and tactical advice to develop a limitless patient flow.**

You don't need a formal $100k education on marketing and business systems; you need a blueprint and a step-by-step checklist! We are so excited to see this opportunity for advanced practice providers right now. From my experience, for every ten private practices, there are seven out there NOT taking advantage of marketing automations or other simple processes that bring your patients back to your clinic, making them excited to engage with you.

The focus of this book is the *patient experience,* because we believe that increased revenue in your practice is a side effect of marketing designed to do what is right for your patients. Delivering excellent care is only one part of the equation. In this book, we'll address the other parts that encompass the patient experience.

Cheers,
Krish Chopra

CHAPTER 1

Marketing Made Easy

"Now more than ever, patients need Advanced Practice Providers as an access point to high quality healthcare. Too many Nurses are struggling in business or worse, never starting due to a lack of education on how to grow a thriving practice."

A Roadmap to What You Will Learn

One of the keys to any successful strategy is to start with a foundation of simple, yet proven methods that obtain results. We have structured this book in a way where each chapter builds upon the preceding chapter—even though tactics may be taken out of order and applied like a user's manual.

We will start the book with some foundational marketing principles, such as creating a unique selling proposition (USP) for your practice and explaining how that can be implemented into your communications to help you stand out from the competition. Then we will explain why having a USP is the "secret sauce" of all successful practices and why most do not have one. We will then cover the three essential avenues every practice owner should maximize to explode revenue generation.

Next, we'll cover the importance of patient engagement and how that can grow the revenue for your practice. We will provide some practical steps and tools for you to leverage to really take your patient engagement to the highest level.

In Chapter 5, we will cover a step-by-step approach to setting up marketing automation for your practice. Once implemented (and we will show you how to do so), this strategy will provide ongoing benefits with minimal time and effort.

We will then explain how to master the patient relationship from a holistic perspective—what to do at every stage of the interaction from the time of scheduling through after they leave your clinic. One challenge that APPs face is figuring out how to create valuable content with minimal time investment. We will cover why this is a challenge and how to easily overcome this in Chapter 7.

As your practice begins to become busier with the use of the strategies and tactics in this book, time becomes even more scarce. Outsourcing can be a tremendous strategy for creating more free time for you to care for patients as your business grows. We will cover how to do this and which tasks are the most common to outsource in practices.

Having an online presence is key to being found by prospective new patients in today's market. We will show you how to get your practice website ranked higher on Google search results using simple search engine optimization (SEO) tactics.

Given the fact that the millennial generation (anyone born between 1980 and 1996) basically grew up with the internet, we wanted to make sure we addressed how to market to this savvy population. So, we've included a chapter entirely dedicated to reaching this demographic.

We've also included an entire bonus chapter on the benefits of precepting and how it can add revenue to your practice as an APP. For each qualified provider, a student can be assigned that can yield up to an additional $10,000 per year.

There is without question a lot of content in this book. So you won't feel overwhelmed, we wanted to create a checklist to follow along with as you read and act. Below is our "Jumpstart" checklist to help serve as a guide as we cover the content in each chapter.

The Jumpstart Checklist

- Create a unique selling proposition (USP)
- Integrate the USP across all of your marketing and communications
- Re-engage with your patient base via email
- Explore strategic alliances to expand your referral network
- Leverage digital marketing with targeted search to attract your ideal patient
- Understand and monitor the "Three Essential Avenues for Revenue Growth"
- Optimize your patient's experience by following the formula in Chapter 4
- Make it easy for patients to find you online and schedule an appointment
- Implement the step-by-step marketing automation found in Chapter 5
- Easily create content and distribute two to three times per week; outsource if necessary
- Implement the "Top 5 Ways to 'WOW' Your Patients" to improve patient loyalty and increase repeat business
- Consider the benefits of outsourcing, which includes hiring a virtual assistant at low cost to help free up your time to serve more patients
- Leverage the recommendations in Chapter 9 to improve how easily prospective patients can find your practice online through search engines such as Google
- If millennials are a vital component of the patient base you serve or want to serve, implement the marketing strategies found in our chapter dedicated to "Marketing to Millennials"
- BONUS: Consider the benefits of precepting as a method to "test drive" future employees, participate in training future providers, and increase the revenue to your practice

A Successful Marketing Strategy

Far too many private practices are struggling or closing because they're not deploying the mindset of a business owner. Our primary goal in writing this book is to provide you with the tools needed to create the attributes of a successful marketing strategy that will help build your flourishing practice.

The key attributes of a successful marketing strategy are:

- Patients should be able to easily interact with my clinic and find me online.
- Be intentional with the patient experience. Recognize that patient care starts before they ever enter the clinic and doesn't end after they leave.
- As a healthcare practitioner, I don't need to become a marketing expert, but I do need to be proactive about my marketing strategy to achieve optimal results.
- If I market my business well, I will have an abundance of patients.
- If I don't market my business well, I won't have many patients.

Our hypothesis is that private practices are closing because they are not operating like successful small businesses. The data supports this as well. <u>The Physicians Foundation</u> conducted a survey of doctors in America and found that 62% of physicians were independent in 2008. By 2014, that number had dropped to 35%, with many accepting offers and buyouts from hospitals or large provider groups.

However, this won't be the case for practices that implement effective strategies, such as those covered in this book. Now that you have this powerful source of information in your hands, let's dive in!

Patience is Key

Keep in mind that like anything worthwhile, the results are not always immediate.

> *How many years did it take to become the type of provider you are now?*

If you stay consistent in applying what's in this book, the results will surpass your expectations. This book can be your answer to understanding how to market your practice, and when executed successfully, it will create consistent growth for your business.

CHAPTER 2

How To Grow Your Practice Without Spending Money On Advertising

"Most practices make the mistake of relying too heavily on referrals and advertising, alone, to grow their revenue."

The Need for Lean Marketing Systems

The amount of money spent on ineffective advertising by practices can be staggering to think about. Unfortunately, most practices have no idea what the return on investment (ROI) is for every dollar spent on advertising the services of their practice. This can be a very frustrating scenario. However, it can be avoided by implementing a lean marketing system that allows for trackable results.

What does it mean to have "lean" marketing? Well, it eliminates all of the wasted spending in your practice on ineffective methods to bring patients through your doors. Most practices spend on advertising methods that include print, local magazines, billboards, radio, mailings, or digital marketing. But before spending a dime on any advertising, a practice can experience significant organic growth by implementing a five-step lean marketing system.

An important question to ask is this: what are you currently spending advertising/marketing dollars on that doesn't allow you to track ROI? If the spend isn't trackable, marketing is like throwing spaghetti against the wall and hoping something will stick. The idea of lean marketing is that everything in place is intentional, trackable, and effective—eliminating waste in your practice.

Overview of the 5-Step Lean Marketing System

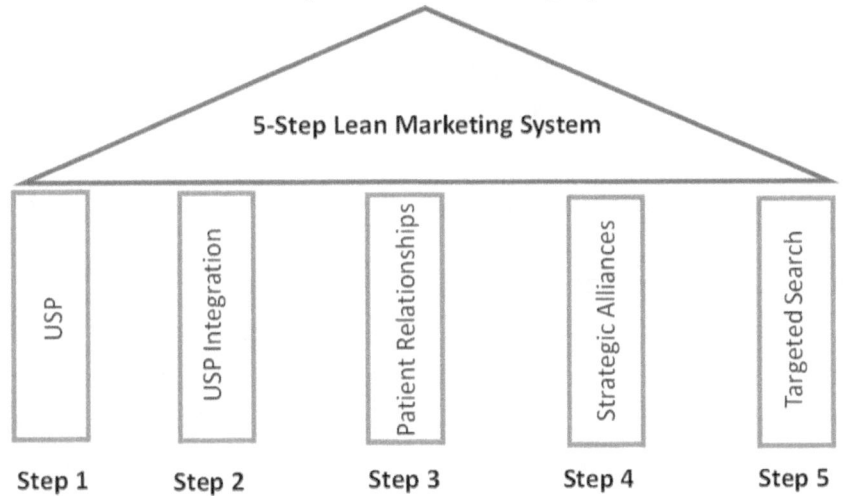

Most practices make the mistake of relying too heavily on referrals and advertising spend to grow their revenue. The 5-step lean marketing system installs a solid foundation for you to grow your practice. Here is an outline of the system:

Step 1: USP.

Create a unique selling proposition (USP) that sets your practice apart from the competition. Your USP should be the foundation of all your marketing efforts—it answers the question: Why should the patient choose to go to your practice? What is the benefit to your patient? You may have the best private practice in your geography, but if you can't communicate what makes it unique, your practice isn't likely to be viewed as a necessity. Without a solid USP, you will have to compete on price of services, and that is a risky strategy for growing revenue.

Depending on the unique characteristics of a private practice, an example of an effective one for a nurse practitioner with many years of experience specializing in women's health could be:

"Join over 20,000 satisfied patients who have trusted XYZ clinic to make women feel better faster without overspending on medical care."

Notice how this USP is built on experience, speed, and cost of care.

This USP leans heavily on the experience of the nurse practitioner and is much more effective than the more common wording of "Over 15 years in business. Choose XYZ Clinic."

Step 2: USP Integration.

Integrating the USP across all marketing materials will ensure that every potential patient receives the same clear message. Does your website have the USP clear and center on the homepage? How are the phones answered in your office? What is written on the walls within the practice? What is on the marketing materials sent to referring providers?

Here is how to ensure the USP created above gets integrated into your practice:

1. It gets communicated on the homepage of your website
2. Employees are educated on the USP and trained to communicate it when patients call to schedule an appointment (if the wording is too long, it can be shortened into a "slogan")
3. All other marketing communications and materials stem from this USP. We don't want to confuse the patient by trying to be all things to all patients!

Step 3: Patient Relationships.

Maintaining patient relationships is built on excellent communication that brings value on an ongoing basis. Patient relationships are really the foundation of a sustainable practice. Think about it: even if you were able to leverage outstanding marketing to bring new patients to your practice, success would fizzle out if they did not return to you at some point in the future. Mastering patient relationships can dramatically reduce your "cost of acquisition," thereby increasing overall profitability to your practice. In other words, building relationships with your patients in a way that gives them real value, either by offering knowledge or solutions, can create tremendous patient loyalty.

One simple way to illustrate this concept is to send a monthly newsletter to your patient base via email that includes tips on staying healthy. Take the common issues you see in your clinic and provide more detail on how to heal faster or prevent the illness altogether. If it is flu season, articulate five steps to preventing the flu. If it is summer, articulate how to recover faster from outdoor activities (recovery from dehydration, sunburn, etc).

Pro Tip: Include an irresistible offer in your newsletter to re-activate your patient base and get them interested in a return visit. For example, you could remind patients to get their flu shot and receive a $20 gift card toward their next visit. Offering ways for patients to return to your practice can really make a difference in their overall well-being.

Step 4: Strategic Alliances.

Build a network of referral sources outside the traditional partnerships. Think about other businesses that serve your ideal patient and how offering your service to them could be a win-win for everyone.

For example, if you specialize in women's health, think about partnering with local gyms or retirement communities to offer ways to prevent common health problems that active women often deal with.

A common way providers can connect with local businesses is to offer free exams, such as at a gym or community center (during busy times). Another way to form local alliances is to identify a handful of local businesses that cater to your target market, such as a church, and ask if you can include an announcement in their newsletter or website that you are accepting new patients in the community. If the local business agrees to share your announcement, include a piece of valuable content to share such as 5 ways to prevent headaches.

The goal is to be seen as a trusted provider and the best way to do that is to deliver valuable content that helps your prospective patients.

Step 5: Targeted Search.

Leverage digital marketing to ramp up the increase in new patient leads for your practice. This step is so much more effective and fruitful after the previous foundational steps are in place. SEO and Facebook ads can be very effective; however, they can be a waste of investment if there is not a solid marketing system in place to convert the "curious clicks" and visibility into loyal patients.

For example, let's say you have a practice focused on women's health located in zip code 30300. The average patient is aged twenty-five to forty-five. A Facebook ad could run to that select market and draw them to your website. Once they are on your website, they will see your USP and have a reason to schedule an appointment with you. If you were to just run ads without creating a USP, traffic would flow to your site but with very low conversions (actual scheduled appointments).

Below is a screenshot of a Facebook Ad used at NP Hub. If someone clicks on this ad, it will take them to a place to schedule an appointment very easily. For your practice, you always want to make it as easy as possible to schedule an appointment. The most common way is to make your phone number easy to find (at the very top, in large font) or include a link to actually pick a time. We find that Contact Forms aren't the most effective in scheduling appointments, largely because it is sometimes a lot of work for the website visitor to fill out.

CHAPTER 3

The Formula For Unlimited Revenue Growth

"Without a USP, private practices risk being perceived as commodities and, as a result, are left to compete on <u>price</u>."

Building on the Secret Sauce of Successful Practices

Like every successful business, private practices need a unique selling proposition (USP)—a reason for the patient to decide to visit YOU versus another provider, versus even not doing anything at all.

Unfortunately, to remain competitive, it's not enough to hang a shingle and provide excellent care. Given the number of options patients have today to seek services or products from well-respected health professionals, you'll need an effective USP to survive and thrive. Below are three reasons why this is so important.

Reason #1: Increase profitability by not reducing price.

Without a USP, private practices risk being perceived as "commodities" and as a result are left to compete on price—offering discounts and eating away at profit margins. Only one private practice in your specialty within your defined market can be the low-price leader. Let's take Wal-Mart as an example of a USP that revolves around being the low-price leader. Now, let's look at Target. Both stores offer comparable products and are often located across the street from each other.

Target and Wal-Mart both offer practically the same products. However, the primary draw for Target shoppers is the customer service aspect and overall shopping environment. The stores have a layout that is a bit easier to navigate and a product selection that covers just about any need.

So, how can Wal-Mart compete with that?

Well, they tend to slightly lower prices ($0.01-0.03 on average), but are able to compete with that since customers who are drawn to Wal-Mart are usually more price-conscious. Both companies thrive and often compete right next door to each other because of their strong USPs. Without a USP, the only way to compete is on price.

Reason #2: Outsmart the competition through differentiation.

A USP gives the patient a clear reason to decide to visit your practice. Maybe it's because you've been in business for twenty years and have served the same local community of over 10,000 patients. Or maybe it's because you are the only practice in your geography that offers a specific cutting-edge technology.

An example of a USP could be: "With over 500 5-star reviews, we continue to help patients in the community relieve their chronic back pain in less than fourteen days and achieve sustainable wellness."

Reason #3: Spend less to acquire new patients with efficient marketing channels.

A well-written USP can dramatically increase your patient conversion rate as well as attract more new patients. When a patient visits your website, there has to be a clearly stated benefit to them in order to have them pick up the phone or schedule an appointment online. One of the biggest mistakes we see today is a private practice sharing information on the website that provides little or no benefit to current or prospective new patients. For example, there may be an entire page on the history of the practice founder, but not much information on the benefits of the services offered. A patient will choose based on USP as well as the knowledge that their problem can be solved. Before publishing any information on the website, ask yourself:

Does the patient really care about this piece of information?
When do patients turn to us for their care?

Just like in sales, a practice has to be able to inform a patient what they can offer to them AND the unique benefit to choosing them as their healthcare provider.

To help craft your very own USP, below are six characteristics to keep in mind that should be part of its development. The important thing to remember is that it likely won't be a "home run" on the first try, so keep reworking based on feedback and results until an effective USP has been developed.

Six Characteristics of a Successful USP:

- Bold
- Specific
- Addresses something that matters to the patient
- Can be confidently delivered upon (it occurs all of the time)
- Difficult to compete with or copy
- Fills a void created by the current market

Three Essential Avenues for Revenue Growth

When it comes to marketing strategy, sticking to the basics can have a dramatic impact on financial performance for your practice. Understanding the following three levers for revenue streams can help organize marketing efforts that will have the greatest impact.

Avenue #1: Number of new patients.

Increase the number of patients coming to your practice with social media.

Creating content and publishing on your website and social media channels is a strong strategy to continuously attract new patients to your practice. Most clinics are not leveraging social media at all, so those who do so effectively will create a competitive advantage.

The key to producing great content is to publish information that would be very useful for your ideal patient. For example, let's say patients often come to you when they have cold symptoms, but they have something worse. Are there a few key indicators patients should know about so they know to schedule an appointment?

Producing valuable content on a weekly basis (at a minimum) will help to establish your practice as an authority in your market.

It can be tempting to be concerned about what is "valuable" to your audience or patient base. One strategy we recommend is observing the questions or concerns from the patients already visiting your practice on a regular basis. What are the common challenges they face? What treatments are they often confused about? Use this information as a springboard for content creation, and your patient base will love you for it.

Avenue #2: Frequency.

Increase the frequency of patient visits to your practice.

A fantastic way that we see increased revenue is by automating communication to your patients, so they get a constant flow of information without asking your staff to do it. A sequential blend of valuable content and special offers through email is a good approach to communicating and strengthening the relationship with your patient base. You can automate this follow-up through high performing email "drip" campaigns (we love using MailChimp or BombBomb).

Additionally, for private practices that provide ongoing services that require follow-up, scheduling the follow-up appointment upon check-out is another way to increase the frequency of patient visits.

Most practices encourage their patients to schedule a follow-up at the front desk as they are leaving the office. Oftentimes, patients leave the office in a hurry and fail to schedule their follow-up appointment. As a result, front desk staff or a scheduler is tasked with calling on that patient at a later point to schedule their follow-up.

Avenue #3: Average revenue per sale.

Increase the average revenue per patient visit.

While increasing the number and frequency of patient visits are important, the revenue per visit is an untapped opportunity. One way to increase this number is to offer patients *additional products or services* that can benefit their acute illness.

For example, if your clinic offers skin treatments, it may be a good idea to keep some of the most popular and effective skin creams in stock to enhance the results of your patient's skin treatments, i.e. an evening wrinkle cream for patients who have just received Botox injections.

The goal when increasing revenue per patient visit should be two-fold: maximize the result for your patient *while* creating additional revenue streams for your practice.

Maximize the hidden assets, such as an <u>existing patient base</u> in your business, with lean marketing strategies in order to grow your business without spending on advertising.

Pro Tip: Many practices tend to focus only on increasing the number of new patients, but increasing the visit *frequency* or *average revenue per patient visit* are surprisingly more beneficial to revenue.

Another business author, Kevin Kelly, coined the phrase "1,000 True Fans," meaning most businesses would be extremely successful if they built 1,000 true fans—this would help grow their business by frequency of patient visits AND number of new patients (through word of mouth).

We believe it's vital for any business to understand the value of one patient to their practice, as this helps keep a perspective on how important each patient is to a thriving practice. Below is a simplified example that can be used to calculate the numbers for your practice. An easy way to calculate average sale is to take total revenue and divide by the total patient appointments in the same time period. For example, let's say last year you brought in $100,000 in revenue and saw 1,000 patients: $100,000/1,000 = $100 per average sale.

Now, in the example below, this $148 average sale translates into a lifetime patient value of $1,332 (oftentimes, this number can be much higher with successful marketing and patient experience)!

Keep in mind the estimates below are very conservative and this number could be much, much greater.

The dollars in your practice are literally driven by the **Inputs** A-E below! The strategies and tactics in this book will help optimize each of these levers:

A. Average sale
B. Number of sales per year per patient
C. Number of years patient buys from you (keep them happy)
D. Number of referrals from patient (WOW them)
E. % Referrals who become patients

Sample Menu of Services	
New Patient Visit	$120
In-Office Procedure	$175
Average Sale	**$148**

Inputs	A. Average Sale =	$148
	B. Number of Sales per year per patient =	2
	C. Number of Years patient buys from you =	4
	D. Number of Referrals from patient =	0.5
	E. % of Referrals who become patients =	0.25
Outputs	F. Gross Sales per year per patient (A x B) =	$296
	G. Gross Sales over life of patient (F x C) =	$1,184
	H. Referrals who become patients (D x E) =	0.125
	I. Gross Sales from referrals (G x H) =	$148
	J. TOTAL VALUE of 1 Satisfied patient (G + I) =	**$1,332**

CHAPTER 4

The Difference Between High Performing Clinics And Mediocre Ones

"Other successful businesses focus on the customer (patient) experience—why don't you?"

Many private practices are not growing every year because they're not taking advantage of the proper systematic hacks that entrepreneurs in other niches are leveraging every day.

If you take the advice in this chapter, your annual revenue could double or even triple in the span of a year.

There are a few key differences as to why certain clinics and certain providers earn well into the millions annually. What are the providers who generate over $2 million per year in revenue doing differently compared to those who struggle to generate just over $250,000?

Here are three of the competitive advantages that are consistently executed by the highest-performing practices.

Advantage #1: Create an Outstanding Patient Experience

Understand that the patient experience doesn't start when they see you, nor does it start when they enter the clinic. It starts when they interact with your website or when they make an appointment.

Clinics that maximize their potential understand the patient experience begins at the first interaction between the clinic and patient, even *before* the patient sets foot in the clinic.

By the time your patient is in the waiting room, they've already interacted with your receptionist and your website. Your patients already have an opinion formed about you and the level of service they're about to receive by the time they enter the exam room.

> **This bears repeating: your patients already have an opinion formed about you before they enter the exam room.**

Here are a few steps to optimize the patient experience:

- Audit your website for ease of scheduling appointments. This is by far the most <u>important</u> function of having a website.
- Leverage a scheduling tool that automatically sends patients confirmation notifications, as well as a way of finding instructions on how to locate your clinic (if necessary).
- If located in a densely populated area, make the parking accommodations clear.
- Streamline the pre-service experience. Can patient registration (demographic and insurance) and intake forms be completed online prior to visit via a patient portal?

Advantage #2: Maximize Every Source of Revenue from the Clinic

Another critical distinction between high-performing clinics and mediocre ones relates to the use of supplemental sources of revenue. In other words, in addition to service revenue, they diversify into additional value-add revenue streams.

There are a few common methods to drive additional income in just under thirty days:

1. Selling complementary products and services on-site at the clinic
2. Speaking engagements (think corporate wellness, colleges, associations, etc.)
3. Precepting medical and nurse practitioner students

Cross-Selling Products/Services

In addition to patient care, successful clinics understand that the patients who are engaging with their clinic want to have more opportunities to improve or optimize their health. Because of this, it can be beneficial for both patients and clinics to offer a wider variety of products and services.

Sometimes providers will resist this idea by saying that they didn't get into medicine to sell products and services, but the reality is that when you see your practice as a business, you want to be able to engage your patients in the way *they* want. This doesn't mean you're doing anything cheap or salesy or not upholding the oath you've taken. All this means is you're **giving your patients what they want**.

In order to gauge what these complementary products and services could be, listen to the requests of your patients or ask them directly.

Other great examples could include partnering with a dietician to put together a few different eating guidelines for your patients who suffer from obesity, or offering sunscreen skin products during the summer months.

Speaking Engagements: Becoming Your Brand

We encourage a lot of clinics with veteran, well-published physicians or nurse practitioners to also consider speaking engagements. At the time of this writing, the world was at the beginning of fighting the Coronavirus pandemic. We suggested that speaking engagements could still be done through video conferencing programs such as Zoom, rather than in-person.

Don't be afraid of building your brand and becoming an industry expert. As a medical provider, you have authority. Your credentials have earned you that. You don't need permission.

Leverage the platforms of social media to engage current and prospective patients. For example, you could set up Instagram, Facebook, and/or Twitter accounts to use as vehicles for your content. Your potential patients are craving insightful, actionable advice from credible sources. If the content adds value to your audience, you will gradually become an authority in your field.

As you become a source of knowledge and build an audience, you can then outreach to potential speaking engagements via email.

Becoming a reliable source of healthcare knowledge will lend itself to becoming your patients' go-to provider when they need your services.

Advantage #3: Marketing Automation Saves Time

Automate your marketing to create a competitive advantage and generate more time to see patients. When you automate your marketing funnel, the process by which prospective patients become returning patients changes everything.

Here's an example of what a *typical low performing* follow-up sequence might look like:

1. A patient works to schedule an appointment with your office either over the phone or through an online portal.
2. 75% of patients come to the appointment. 25% of patients cancel the day of the appointment or the day before. Many patients also arrive late.
3. After their appointment, they go home without speaking or engaging with the receptionist.

Unfortunately, this is what we have seen most clinics do. There are several critical components missing here.

As a business owner, every new patient is an opportunity to create a lifelong patient. In entrepreneurship, this is known as LTV (life-time value).

As opposed to the basic methods outlined above, a more in-depth and personalized strategy for encouraging repeat patients would look like this:

1. The day the patient books their appointment, they get an automatic email addressed to their first name, thanking them for booking the appointment, along with an embedded video from the provider welcoming them to their first visit. This video can be thirty seconds long.
2. Then, on the day of the appointment, they receive a reminder text message and/or email.
3. Patient arrives on time (reduces "no-show" rate).
4. After the appointment, they get a thank-you email and a recap of the services they received, including a summary of what to do next. **Note: You could craft most of these messages for 80% of the most common diagnoses and treatment plans fairly easily.**
5. A week later, the patient receives a one-minute survey on the care they received and a video series of golden nuggets to follow to stay healthy during flu or back-to-school season.

Here is the good news: ninety percent of the above steps can happen automatically, and we'll show you how to set it up.

CHAPTER 5

Step-By-Step Marketing Automation

"Successful marketing requires some element of testing to see how well your patients respond to the pains and desires that you perceive them to have."

In the past ten years, the business landscape has changed. Rather than building a team where each person is hyper-specialized, we're seeing more small businesses have one person who can fit multiple roles. The only way this has been possible is by automating and outsourcing certain tasks.

The key to successful marketing automation is to follow a simple sales conversion methodology.

In your practice, this would begin once a potential new patient visits your website and decides to opt-in to receive content.

Example of Marketing Automation

In this scenario, let's say a new patient has found your website and decided to sign-up (or commonly called opt-in) to receive your monthly newsletter. Here is what would occur:

Touch Point 1: Thank You Message

a. **Medium for Message:** *Email only OR Email & Text*
b. **When should a message be triggered?** *Immediately*
c. **Sample Subject Line:** *Thank You For Subscribing!*
d. **Sample Email Template:**

> *Hi [Insert Name]!*
>
> *Thank you for visiting our website and joining our monthly newsletter! Here are some tips on how to stay healthy during flu season.*
>
> *Have questions? We have answers! Feel free to reply to this email to get in touch with us or schedule an appointment by clicking here or calling 123-456-9876.*
>
> *Thank You,*
> *[Insert Provider's Name]*

Touch Point 2: Value Add Message

a. **Medium for Message:** *Email*
b. **When should a message be triggered?** *One Week Later*
c. **Sample Subject Line:** *How To Treat [Insert Common Ailment] this Season*
d. **Sample Email Template:**

> Hi [first name],
>
> We're seeing a lot of patients coming into the clinic with [common ailment of the season]. Here's a quick two-minute video on the five keys to caring for your [common ailment].
>
> To schedule your annual wellness visit (usually 100% covered by your insurance), please visit our appointment portal here, or call XXX-XXX-XXXX.
>
> We have a current window to accept new patients. [insert USP].

Touch Point #3: Appointment Confirmation

a. **Medium:** *Email and/or Text*
b. **When should a message be triggered?** *Immediately when an appointment is booked*
c. **Sample Subject Line:** *Thank you for scheduling your appointment on X date/time*
d. **Sample Email Body:**

> *Hi [first name],*
>
> *Your appointment is confirmed!*
> *Please review the email below.*
>
> *Below is the information we received from the form you filled out.*
> *[List information]*
>
> *We look forward to [insert USP] on X date and time.*
>
> *Warm regards,*
> *[Provider Name]*

Note: Include a picture of you and your clinic team to increase familiarity and begin to build trust.

Sample text message for appointment confirmation:

> *Hi [Name]! We look forward to seeing you today at [insert date and time for their appointment]. Call our office with any questions you may have.*
> *Address/Suite #*
> *Parking instructions*
> *Arrival time*

We recommend using Avochato (https://www.avochato.com) to get started with text messaging.

We are huge advocates of texting patients because texting has a 99% open rate, meaning you can basically guarantee your patient is reading your message even if they don't reply, whereas emails may get lost in their inbox.

Pro Tip: If you leverage the power of text messaging in your business, make sure to give your patients the option of opting out at ANY time.

This is just one possible example of automation that can save you time and help automatically convert the traffic on your website to more patient appointments.

1. Email: Continue Adding Value Bi-Weekly

Even if the patient does not sign up for an appointment, communication should still be maintained.

A cadence we recommend is to "give, give, give, ask, repeat." For the first three emails, you are giving pure high-quality information that is of interest to your patient base; then you make an offer for an appointment on the third or fourth.

If you'd like to learn more about this method of communication, Gary Vaynerchuk's *Jab, Jab, Jab, Right Hook* is an excellent resource. Gary Vaynerchuk is the chairman of VaynerX, a modern-day media and communications holding company, and the active CEO of VaynerMedia, a full-service advertising agency servicing Fortune 100 clients across the company's four locations.

Are Marketing Automations Common in Private Practices?

Not really.

Believe it or not, some practices don't even have a functioning website. The practices that do have a website usually don't have an easy way for patients to schedule appointments. Instead, they are only given a number to call the office.

This process is incredibly inefficient because it creates an additional barrier to entry for your potential patients. Clients today don't have the same level of patience as they did in 1995.

In fact, a 2015 study done by Zocdoc indicated that 24% of

Americans have trouble booking an appointment, and when they need to reschedule, 26% wait several weeks to reschedule.

If a potential new patient is on hold for more than thirty seconds or can't schedule an appointment after business hours, we promise you they're likely not calling again.

The key to increasing revenue via automation is making it simple for patients to reach you, and this includes an online scheduling function. This is not a "Contact Us" form. Instead, online scheduling gives the patient visibility into actual availability and allows them to find a time that works best for them.

Another example of automation is what happens after a patient has received treatment.

Next Steps

Answer the following questions.

1. **In a perfect world, what should happen when a patient leaves your clinic?**
2. **What are your next three touchpoints with each patient?**

Because you've committed to reading and implementing the effective strategies in this book, you understand touch-points no longer need to be manual.

Here's an example of an engaging post-visit email:

Subject Line: Summary of Patient Experience - [Insert Patient Full Name]

Dear Patient A,

Thank you for visiting Get Well Clinic on (today's date).

We hope the time you spent with Dr. X will help you feel better soon.

Today, you came in expressing sensitivity to light, fatigue, and migraine symptoms. With the migraine you are experiencing, we recommend drinking plenty of fluids, getting adequate rest (at least seven hours), and avoiding bright lights in the evening hours. The prescription for your migraine medication should be available at the pharmacy now.

If you do not begin to feel better in three days, please give our office a call at 123-456-7890 and ask to speak with a nurse, or you can book a follow up appointment with this link.

[Insert Custom Link Here]

You may also message us directly through the patient portal at any time.

We are here to help you feel better as quickly as possible.

From time to time, you may have some questions regarding your health and staying healthy. Please check out our weekly newsletter at [Insert Link]. Dr. X updates it weekly, answering the most popular questions she received that week.

> *Warm regards,*
> *Your Healthcare Team at Get Well Clinic*
>
> *P.S. The newsletter is also updated on Facebook for weekly tips on being healthy. Follow us on Facebook here! [Insert Link]*

This is an excellent example of a follow-up email. Now, let's deconstruct the components of this email.

Components of Follow-up Email:

1. Personalization
2. An expression of gratitude for their time
3. Summary of appointment
4. Treatment Summary
5. A new link to schedule their next appointment
6. Links to the website's latest blog posts to keep in touch about their wellness
7. A Facebook page link

What wasn't included in this email that can be added?

Some providers offer a form template that summarizes the patient's experience during the appointment—below is a sample of the type of information to include and an example form template:

a. Patient Name
b. Date of Service
c. Provider Name
d. Diagnosis
e. Treatment Summary

f. What to do if condition does not improve
g. Other information that may help with condition
h. A link to schedule follow-up appointment

A Note to Remember

Your patients want the level of service outlined above. Right now, private practices are failing in this regard. This is why the opportunity to start a new practice is so incredible.

If you implement half of the content in this chapter, you'll be light-years ahead of other practices in your immediate area.

With the ever-decreasing barriers to entry, think of your service as a commodity. Patients can go to any other clinic in the city and receive the same service, but they choose to come to you. With this mindset, you can spark the creativity necessary to be innovative and provide a higher level of service.

Pro Tip: Remember to send emails that are HIPAA compliant if they contain any patient information. A partner we recommend to ensure emails are compliant without any extra steps is paubox.com.

> The key to successful marketing automation is
> to follow a simple sales conversion methodology.

Emailing Patients with an Offer: The Devil is in the Details

A few small tweaks to your marketing communication can often have a dramatic impact on your revenue growth.

So far, we have shown how utilizing marketing and automation can have a dramatic impact on building your patient base and relationships. However, we have found that there are three very common and detrimental mistakes that private practices make when making an offer via email to their patient base. See if you can **spot the mistakes** in the example below:

We love our patients at ABC Dermatology.

Our cosmetic services will help you reduce the effects of aging and achieve your perfect skin. As a thank-you for being our patient, we have a special offer just for you.

A few of the skin problems a cosmetic service will solve are:

- *wrinkles*
- *droopy eyelids*
- *scars*
- *age or liver spots*

Give us a call today!

Sincerely,
ABC Dermatology Team
ABC Dermatology, a trusted affiliate of XYZ Health System

Example Revised:

> Turn back the clock of time with safe and effective skin treatments from your local dermatologist with over 15,000 satisfied patients. } **Mistake #1** Remind them of your USP
>
> Our cosmetic services will help you reduce the effects of aging and achieve your perfect skin. As a thank you for being our patient, we have a special offer just for you.
>
> Call before July 13, 201X to schedule ANY cosmetic service and receive a 10% discount on the total cost of your appointment, along with a FREE gift ($175 value). } **Mistake #2** Be specific with the offer
>
> A complete list of our cosmetic services can be found on our website, here.
>
> A few of the skin problems a cosmetic service will solve are:
>
> - wrinkles
> - droopy eyelids
> - scars
> - age or liver spots
>
> Call the friendly team with ABC Dermatology at 123-456-7890 or click here to schedule online immediately! } **Mistake #3** Not having a clear "Call to Action"
>
> Sincerely,
>
> ABC Dermatology Team
> ABC Dermatology, a trusted affiliate of XYZ Health System

In summary, three of the most common mistakes are:

- **Mistake #1**: Not including your unique selling proposition (USP) in the body of the email communication. Otherwise, why should they pay attention to what you are offering?
- **Mistake #2**: Not being specific with the offer. Avoid being vague here. Tell them exactly what is in it for them. Is it to save 10% off the total cost of the appointment?
- **Mistake #3**: Not having a clear call to action. In other words, what action would you like the reader to take after reading the email? Be clear and make it easy for them to follow-through.

The above example is a good formula for making an offer to a patient, but these must be tested with your patient base in order to determine if they are effective.

Successful marketing requires some element of testing to see how well your patients respond to the pains and desires that you perceive them to have. The key is to keep track of what works and what doesn't, through A-B testing.

A-B testing is basically changing only one element in a second "B" test, or variation test, while keeping the other "A" test, or control, unchanged. For example, we could change the above subject line of the email, keeping everything else the same, and then see if that impacts the email open rate. An easy way to do this is to send one email (A test) to fifty percent of your patients and the other (B test) to the other fifty percent of your patients, then see which set of emails gets opened more.

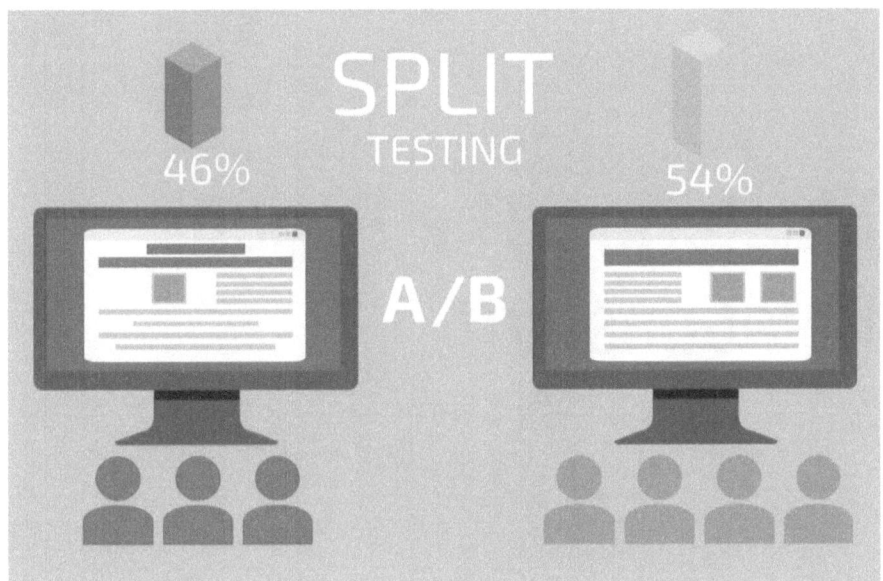

Again, if we can't measure the marketing activity, then it is likely going to be difficult to assess the return of that effort.

So, we've seen how making an offer could work via email, or we've at least covered the essential components of a well-constructed offer. Now, we will see how easy it can be to create valuable content for your patients that will help nurture the relationship over time.

CHAPTER 6

Mastering The Patient Relationship

"Nothing shows a patient you care about them more than calling to check on them, even for a minute."

Most private practices fail to communicate with their patient base after they leave the clinic and risk losing a valuable lifelong relationship.

However, most practices could easily maintain a flourishing patient base by mastering a few communication tactics that help to create an exceptional patient experience.

As we saw in the last chapter, setting up marketing automation via email and text can be beneficial to continuously nurture patient rapport. In this chapter, we will see additional tactics outside of automation that can help improve the patient relationship and create raving fans.

Increase Repeat Business with Excellent Service: Top 5 Ways to "Wow" Your Patients

In our experience, there are private practices that excel at patient satisfaction with the way they choose to "WOW" their patients on a regular basis.

Here are five of the best recommendations we've heard from high-performing clinics that can be implemented immediately:

1. Call after treatment

This is especially true for NEW patients. You want to make them feel welcomed and valued as a patient to your practice.

At the end of a full day of seeing patients, it can be hard to want to pick up the phone and call the patients you saw that day. However, nothing shows a patient you care about them more than calling to check on them, even for a minute. If you do this, it will differentiate you almost instantly from the 99% of providers who do not. How likely will the patient be to recommend you to their family and friends if they know they will be treated with this level of service?

Pro Tip: If you simply don't have the time, you can ask a staff member to make these calls. However, there is a certain degree of caring that comes through to the patient when their own provider calls to check on them.

2. Avoid convoluted phone trees

Nobody wants to press 1 for English or 14 to speak with an operator. Having a live person answer the phone almost immediately (within three rings), will set you apart from the competition. If you don't have the staffing available to do this, you can hire a high quality and affordable virtual assistant from companies such as Fiverr, Upwork, or Outsource Access.

3. Maximize the waiting room experience

While patient wait times should be limited as much as possible, it is valuable to enhance their experience while they wait. For example, have updated magazines and periodicals available for them to read—if there are issues from 2005 sitting around, it won't support your image of providing an excellent experience. Additionally, you could record videos of yourself to play in the waiting room for your patients—the content could be educational or inspirational.

Even some of the smallest tweaks can go a long way in improving the waiting room experience. For example, offering a small water cooler or free beverage options to be available in the waiting room for patients to access while they wait can create a much more welcoming feel to the practice.

4. Communication is King

As noted earlier in the book, a key component of the patient experience is when they contact your office to make an appointment and should continue after they leave with valuable information via email and social media. In the next chapter, we will discover how to create content very easily without taking too much time.

If you're too busy to call the patient after their first visit, another simple communication strategy is to send handwritten thank-you notes to every *new patient* after their very first visit to your office. This lets them know they are valued and you recognize they have a choice in private practice.

Pro Tip: If you can include something you actually spoke about with the patient in the thank-you note, it will create a strong connection with them. For example, if you learned they are taking an upcoming vacation, tell them to enjoy their trip. Personal touches like this are almost non-existent in healthcare; this is just one way you can differentiate your private practice. Doing this will help you build a lifelong relationship and become their trusted, go-to provider.

5. Professionalism of Office Staff

Having your staff wear uniforms (or similar style clothing, i.e. business casual) and creating a welcoming environment for patients will set your office apart. Many office settings have the "Top 40" blasting on the radio as the patient walks through the office to their treatment room. Music is okay, but it shouldn't be overbearing. Otherwise, it could communicate to the patient that they are not the focus of the experience and someone's dance party is more important.

Pro Tip: To optimize the patient experience for your practice, an approach that we recommend is to walk through the entire patient interaction from their perspective and try to communicate in a way that (1) anticipates needs, (2) makes the interaction seamless, and (3) manages the emotional states of the patient during each step of the process.

CHAPTER 7

How to Create Content Easily

"When deciding on topics to discuss, just consider the most common ailments or questions you see daily from patients. The common ailments that your patients are fighting present a treasure chest of helpful content worth creating."

One of the most popular questions in practice marketing is: How do I create content easily that is high quality and will benefit my patients?

It can seem complicated, especially between coming up with topics and video-editing.

As providers and practice managers, you don't have an hour or two each day to create content. In fact, just thinking about that may seem like a waste of your valuable time.

This chapter is the answer.

As we saw in Chapter 4, the patient experience starts when they first interact with you on social media or on your website, not when they come into your clinic for their appointment.

> **Don't be surprised if, after starting video content, when you first greet new patients, they refer to your videos.**

At that point, they've already formulated their opinion about you.

Let's repeat that: by the time a patient presents themselves at your clinic, they've already formulated a first impression or opinion of how the experience will go.

Right now, most practices are not creating content, which is an oversight and provides a huge opportunity for a high performer like you. People are interacting with video, blogs, and content on a scale we've never seen before. When you're not creating content, you're becoming just another practice, essentially just another commodity.

Common Reasons Providers Don't Produce Videos

"I don't have a professional camera."

Many practitioners believe erroneously that videos can only be high-quality if recorded with a professional camera, but this is no longer true! Smartphones are more than sufficient for recording.

With a simple tripod and mic, quality content is more attainable than ever—not to mention, recording on your phone shows a level of authenticity that your patients will relate to. In fact, many patients are turned off by "perfectly recorded" content because it does not come across as authentic.

A simple and useful tripod can be found for as little as $14 by doing a search on Amazon. It can be found by typing this address into your browser: https://amzn.to/2MaBWqh.

As for sound quality, we recommend a valuable mic on Amazon for $13. It can be found by typing this address into your browser: https://amzn.to/2MbMMMC.

"I don't have the time."

Yes, it can take some time in the beginning to record videos. Sometimes, to record a two- to three-minute video, you may need two to three attempts. But, as you become more consistent, a two- to three-minute video will take just two to three minutes.

When you're recording, please remember these three things, which will help you create with urgency.

1. The number of patients (now and in the future) that could benefit from your message.
2. If this video isn't perfect, that's perfectly okay. After all, you have a new video coming later this week.
3. Don't judge the video by the number of followers or likes. EVERYONE started with zero followers.

If you truly don't have the time, you can hire a videographer to record videos for you, edit them, and repurpose each video into multiple pieces of content. Many practices do this and create amazing content.

For example, while not a nurse practitioner, one dentist at Constantine Dental created a short forty-second video. It went viral (over 800,000 likes), and they have been scheduling clients left and right! The simple video example can be found by typing this address in your browser: https://bit.ly/2LmnhvV.

We've probably been asked three hundred times on what should be included in the first recorded video. We recommend starting with a one-minute video discussing *why* you opened your practice.

When it comes time to share your knowledge with the world, there are just two simple steps we recommend. First, upload your video to YouTube, then post on various media channels such as Instagram and Facebook for maximum visibility. Leverage hashtags for words that may commonly be searched for when finding your video.

The Krish Chopra Hack to Creating Content

In the beginning stages of your business, it can be time-intensive to create content. Between recording videos, editing, social media posting, caption writing, SEO optimization, and more, it's no wonder why marketing is such a popular career choice.

When you first get started, you may not have the budget ready to commit to hiring a team of content creators.

While content creation can seem like a full-time job, there are a few ways to ease the burden on constantly creating content. The key is to repurpose content. Please understand that one piece of content can be used anywhere between five and ten times.

How? Practice owners can record one piece of content and repurpose the same content for different platforms. We will walk through exactly how to do this.

Here's the step-by-step guide to creating compelling content.

Step 1: Record a Video

For example, if you're a primary care provider, you can discuss tactics to avoid getting sick in the fall. If you're a women's health provider or OB/GYN, you can discuss a few ways to reduce discomfort in your first trimester.

Remember you're the healthcare expert. When deciding on topics to discuss, a great place to start is to consider the most common ailments or questions you've seen from patients in the past month.

As a provider, people want to know your opinions and engage with you. When you post content on social media, you're engaging with both your current and future patients.

Once the content is on video, it's time for Step 2.

Step 2: Get Your Video Transcribed (for cheap!)

To take the video content and produce text, we recommend Temi or Speechpad, but there are at least twenty other options that do the same thing for you. When you get your videos transcribed, you've now completed 75% of the work. The best part is this is extremely cost effective—it takes less than $3–$8 per video. When you receive your finished transcription, all that needs to be done is quick editing. Depending on your editing speed, this can take a maximum of fifteen minutes for a three-minute video.

You can even outsource this editing task (more on outsourcing in the next chapter) to make your life easier. Now you can have a writer or assistant convert the transcription into text that can be used as a blog post for your website.

Typically, the main responsibility involved for the writer is to remove all the filler words, such as "um" and "like," and refine the colloquialism. This allows you to repurpose original, high-value content easily. To take the video content and produce text, we recommend using either Temi (www.temi.com) or Speechpad (www.speechpad.com). You could also find this service on Fiverr or Upwork and send them the video for transcription. This is usually very affordable (less than $15 in most cases).

Step 3: Videos Allow the Written Blog to be in "Your Voice"

The best part is you don't have to worry about the writing style resembling your voice because the video was made by you, in your own voice. This is an incredibly powerful trick that removes the arduous work that comes with creating and writing blog posts. If you have some initial trouble recording a video comfortably, try using a short script that outlines talking points. Comfort with video comes over time, with practice.

By the time you've recorded your tenth video, you'll be amazed at how far you've come.

Step 4: Post Both the Video and Blog on Social Media

Once you have a video produced and transcribed, you have the completed content to post onto social media and your blog. Additionally, you do not need to post all of the content at once. For example, you could divide the key points into "bite-sized" posts that could be shared over a few weeks.

Step 5: Use the Vocabulary Your Patients Will be Familiar With (vs. medical jargon)

When creating content and describing it in your posts, make sure you do a keyword analysis to find the words your potential patients are using on search platforms like Google, Bing, etc.

How to do a simplified keyword analysis:

1. Go to your favorite search engine, like Google.
2. Think of a phrase your potential patients might use in their search.
3. Type a phrase in Google and see what sentences populate quickly.

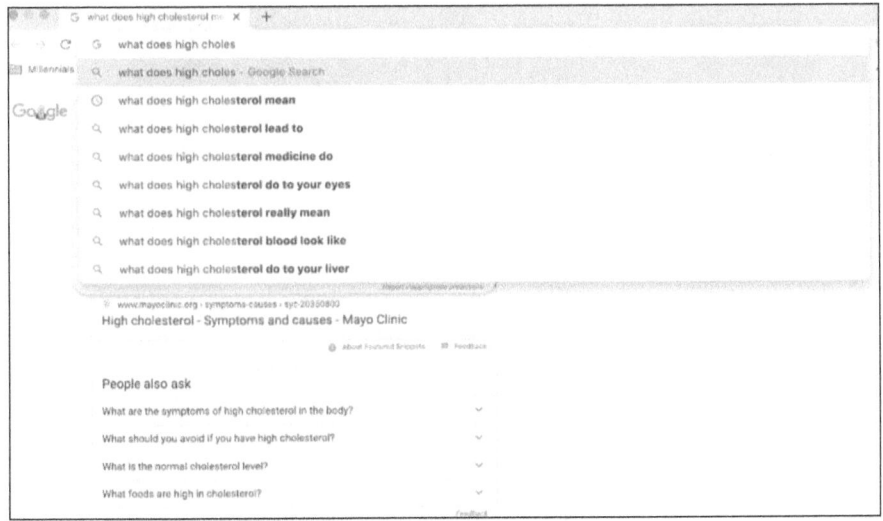

©2018 Google LLC, used with permission. Google and the Google logo are registered trademarks of Google LLC.

1. Scroll to the bottom and see related searches.

> **Searches related to what does high cholesterol mean**
>
> high cholesterol **treatment**
> what **are the symptoms of** high cholesterol **in the body**
> **causes of** high cholesterol **in healthy person**
> high cholesterol **symptoms eyes**
> high cholesterol **symptoms fatigue**
> cholesterol **test**
> what **is** cholesterol
> cholesterol **diet**
>
> Goooooooooogle >
> 1 2 3 4 5 6 7 8 9 10   Next

©2018 Google LLC, used with permission. Google and the Google logo are registered trademarks of Google LLC.

Don't use the medical terms for illnesses. If your average patient wouldn't recognize the word, do not use it. This is critical for Search Engine Optimization (SEO), which we will explore in Chapter 9.

CHAPTER 8

The Incredible Benefits Of Outsourcing

"If someone is calling your clinic to schedule an appointment, they are looking for a human experience—not being placed on hold for two minutes."

While there's a lot of tactical advice for implementing outsourcing in your practice, one of the biggest benefits we see is in the *virtual receptionist arena*.

As we briefly discussed with Chapter 6 on Mastering the Patient Communication, one of the biggest challenges in any busy clinic is that every employee is pulled in fifteen different directions. Therefore, when answering phones for new patients, it's critical they do not wait long. However, most prospective patients are put on hold for thirty seconds to two minutes.

In today's hyper-impatient society, when you place a first-time caller or prospective patient on hold, you're already hurting the patient experience with the initial interaction. Good luck recovering from that.

If someone is calling your clinic to schedule an appointment, they're looking for a human experience—not being placed on hold for two minutes.

Even if your practice is busy, you cannot afford to alienate your prospective patients unintentionally. Your patients should feel that their provider cares and has their best interest at heart.

Believe it or not, this begins by reducing the friction to schedule an appointment and answering the phone promptly.

How Outsourcing Can Help

Scheduling Appointments

Hire a virtual assistant to be the receptionist, so when you have an inbound call, the caller can speak to a real human.

For hiring virtual assistants, we recommend going on **Fiverr, Upwork, or Outsource Access** to find high-quality, low-cost virtual assistants who will be able to fill the need to schedule patients promptly. Just head over to Fiverr (https/:www.fiverr.com) or Upwork and search for "virtual assistant."

Think of the impact this has on your revenue: your schedule is a huge driver of that revenue, so tactics that enhance this capability are a good strategy to adopt.

Before hiring the virtual assistant, you can spend an hour with them teaching them about your practice, patients, and scheduling protocol. To ensure scheduling accuracy with your virtual assistant or multiple staff members, we recommend creating a simple one-page Standard Operating Procedure (SOP) for scheduling patients.

The benefits of investing this time are huge when it comes to enhancing the patient experience through scheduling via virtual assistants.

Sending Follow-Up Emails

In Chapter 5, we outlined marketing automations and follow-up procedures to help ensure that your patients have a great experience.

Another time-consuming task that can be outsourced is email writing.

In this case, at the end of the day or after each patient leaves, you can send your assistant a voice note outlining the follow-up email to send the patient. Creating leverage with your time is absolutely necessary as your practice grows. These days, you can record voice notes directly in texting platforms like Messenger, WhatsApp, and texting applications.

Make sure your assistant documents the email templates for each new patient case. Over time, you'll have more templates ready for use.

CHAPTER 9

Simple Search Engine Optimization (SEO) Practices To Rank Higher On Google

"One important key when writing anything on your website is to use jargon that your patients use, not the jargon common in the medical profession."

What is SEO?

Search engine optimization, or SEO, is the process of ranking higher on search results using platforms like Google or Bing in order to get more "organic" or "free" website visitor traffic.

The key to SEO is strategically encrypting your content with keywords that will improve its search ranking.

SEO can become complicated quickly, but we will highlight 70% of the basics that will help set you apart from many practices that aren't utilizing these strategies.

In our experience, the best SEO strategies leverage videos and blogging, as they're the most consumed content format.

Why Blogging?

Blogging takes advantage of search engine optimization (SEO) on platforms like Google search.

Typical blog posts should be between 750 to 1500 words in length. When you create keyword-rich content (based on your prospective patient's searches), search engines will start recognizing your website as an authority on the subject.

Why Videos?

A study done by Cisco indicated that by the end of 2022, online videos will make up more than 82% of all consumer internet traffic—fifteen times higher than it was in 2017. Not only that, but the videos have the most engagement on social media channels and are the most commonly shared content.

Best Practices to be Found Through SEO

Video → Blog Transcription

One of the best practices, as we saw in Chapter 7, comes into play here once again. Creating videos, transcribing them, and then turning that content into a blog post can really boost SEO results. The below example is in the context of SEO:

Let's say you are a private practice nurse practitioner who wants to attract patients to your clinic. Think of the most common pain points your patients share with each other (maybe acne or visible wrinkles).

For this example, you can make a video about the specific foods that contribute to acne and how some basic preventative measures can be taken to reduce its severity.

In the video, make sure to use the variations of keywords related to "acne" many times for the best SEO benefits.

Examples of variations
- The best acne treatments are
- Home remedies for acne
- How to remove acne without scarring
- How to get rid of acne overnight

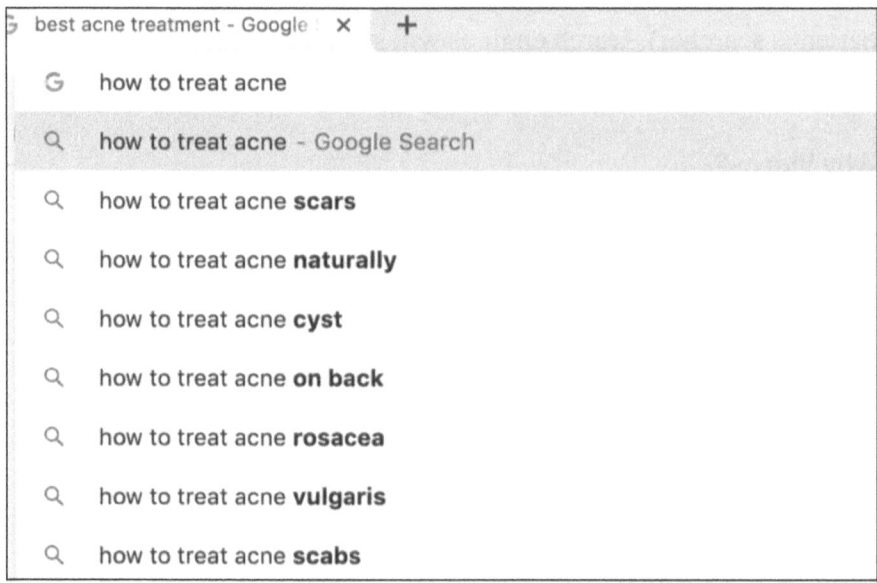

©2018 Google LLC, used with permission. Google and the Google logo are registered trademarks of Google LLC.

Content Collaboration

There are far too many providers right now who aren't producing highly valuable content, let alone collaborating with peers. A good approach to take to find a collaborator is to look at adjacent professions. If someone goes to a dentist, they also need to go to the doctor, right?

This concept is known as "working in adjacent industries."

An example in this case could be a podiatrist and women's health combination. If a patient visits a women's health specialist, there's a likelihood they may experience foot pain due to their pregnancy. This presents a perfect opportunity for content collaboration. This collaboration could set the foundation for future referral opportunities. Patients visiting the women's health specialist with foot pain could be referred to the podiatrist. Patients with foot pain who are pregnant could be referred to the women's health specialist.

These opportunities are present in every kind of small business, so practices would be astute to follow suit and begin collaborations with adjacent industries.

Another approach for content collaboration is with an old friend or classmate. A common message we advise our clients to send is:

Dear Dr/Mr/Miss _____,

My name is _____, and I'm a provider with _____. I'm reaching out to you because I really admire the work your practice does and feel we could benefit from a partnership!

There's a lot of overlap between the needs of my _____ patients and your _____ patients, and I think we could both gain a lot of traction by creating a short video together that addresses some potential

> *patient questions and concerns. This video could be used as a marketing tool on our blogs, websites, and social media.*
>
> *Look forward to exploring a mutually beneficial project together—let me know if you are interested by calling me at 123-456-9876.*

Keyword Rankings on Search Engines

When you are creating content, make sure you're using the keywords that people search for. We discussed this with the "acne" example.

Use the jargon your patients use, not the jargon your specialty uses. Using jargon to demonstrate your knowledge is a common mistake practitioners make because patients won't usually understand what is being said. Therefore, keeping the language in a format that a third-grader could understand will have the greatest reach and influence.

A simple tool to use is the SEMRUSH (www.semrush.com) keyword planner. SEMRUSH is an SEO tool that does your keyword research, tracks the keyword strategy used by competitors, and runs an SEO audit of your blog. This tool pulls all of the terms that people search for on a specific topic.

CHAPTER 10

Marketing To Millennial Patients

"It's imperative to realize that appealing to this age group is vastly different from appealing to an aging patient population, such as the baby-boomer generation."

We are all well aware of the "baby-boomer" generation and their need for healthcare services. However, we wanted to include a chapter on how to reach millennials, as this age group (born 1981–1996) is among the fastest growing and presents an opportunity to increase lifetime value, as we discussed earlier in the book.

Providers need to realize that many millennials are now in their thirties, as patient care moves younger and younger toward millennials and even Generation Z (anyone born after 1997).

To attract millennial patients, you need to have an online presence! Millennials don't prefer to talk to businesses over the phone. They want to be able to engage on their own time, typically over mobile devices. This also runs true for Generation Z, who are now in their young twenties.

There are three necessary components to market to millennials:

1. Social media
2. Online reviews
3. A well-put-together website

Let's dive into each of these three different methods to make sure your clinic is optimized to attract more patients.

The Importance of Social Media

Social media is everywhere, and that means your current and future patients are paying attention to it. Creating content on social media is the equivalent to having a TV commercial in 1980. In 1980, when American families would watch TV together after work, commercials were the best way to win the consumer's attention.

In today's times, people spend up to seven hours a day on their phone. This is why business owners need to go to where the attention is focused.

Social media platforms are the new TV channels. Facebook is NBC, Instagram is ABC, LinkedIn is CNN, Youtube is CBS, and Google is the TV Guide channel!

This means actively posting at least *once per week* on these platforms in the beginning, then producing as frequently as once per day. This also means being actively involved and communicating with your followers and your page fans through the use of likes, comments, and content.

Which Platforms Matter

1. Facebook
2. Instagram
3. LinkedIn
4. Google My Business
5. YouTube

Facebook and Instagram

Now, obviously this means that you must have a page for your practice on Facebook, period. It takes about ten minutes to create a page for your practice. Once you have a page, you can post content, invite friends/family to like it, and include a link on the bottom of email signatures.

We recommend including the following items on your page:

- Name of practice
- Location/Address
- Phone number
- Website or scheduling link

Chapter 10: Marketing To Millennial Patients

You must also have an Instagram account. Instagram has been one of the fastest growing platforms in recent years, which means your millennial patient is likely on Instagram!

Facebook is aging upward, meaning the older population is using Facebook more frequently, while younger people are shifting to Instagram.

LinkedIn

Most practices aren't creating a simple "Company Page" on LinkedIn but are missing out on the exposure it provides. LinkedIn is a great way to engage professionals and has incredible organic reach. That means that more people are likely to see your posts than compared with Facebook and Instagram because there is much less competition for content.

Creating a company page that can be attached to your LinkedIn profile takes only a few minutes. Posting content here is key for exposure to prospective patients as well as potential business partners.

How to Have an Active Google Listing

Google My Business is game-changing for your practice! It's not quite social media, but remember, Google is today's TV guide.

Make sure your Google listing is activated because all people use Google. And people Google everything! When a potential patient Googles "primary care clinic near me" you want to make sure your listing pops up near the top!

Do I Need to Leverage YouTube?

YouTube is a great aggregator of videos. Make sure any content you ever produce is uploaded to YouTube. YouTube is owned by Google, so having a proper YouTube channel and YouTube post (header, description, meta-tags, etc.) will help you show up on Google searches.

The specific details of a great YouTube video post are out of the scope of this book, but lots of details can be found on the web.

Tools to Schedule Posts in Advance

Staying active with Facebook, Instagram, and LinkedIn posts can become time-consuming. However, there is a simple platform that helps you save time by pre-loading posts to be posted live at scheduled times. A tool used at NPHub is Smarter Queue, which allows us to schedule posts weeks in advance. This way, when a trip or a last-minute emergency arises, you already have posts ready to go.

Advanced: Running Social Media Ads

An advanced strategy talked about in Chapter 2 is to get involved in running social media ads on Facebook, Instagram, LinkedIn, and/or Google. Creating ads can be quite complex and out of the scope of this book, but it's worth investing time and resources if the marketing fundamentals discussed in Chapter 2 are in place.

There's a massive ROI to running effective ads to generate new patient traffic and even new patient appointments. Once you accomplish the first three strategies above and are ready to hire a social media marker, we recommend turning your focus to paid advertising to grow your practice even more. There is a lot of nuance to running social media ads, so it's typically best to find a consultant. Without the proper coding and tracking implemented, it will be impossible to measure ROI on ad spend.

Online Reviews

According to a study by Planet Marketing, 90% of customers first check online reviews prior to making a purchase. If you ask the typical healthcare business owner, they'll tell you they know reviews are important. But two common challenges always arise.

Challenge #1: Where Do I Need Reviews?

There are many different platforms where reviews are needed. Between Google, Yelp, Facebook, Healthgrades, and ZocDoc, determining which platform to start with and how to manage the reviews can be overwhelming.

The key is to focus on one platform at a time and to start with Google. Once you have fifteen reviews on Google, then move to Facebook, then to Healthgrades, ZocDoc, etc.

Challenge #2: How Do I Constantly Get Reviews?

Anytime you have a new patient leaving your clinic, ask them for a very quick review on Google. If they're a happy patient, there's a very high chance they will say yes.

Sample Script: "Do you mind doing a quick Google review for us? It would really mean a lot to our clinic and future patients."

If you feel uncomfortable asking for a review, you can train your office manager or receptionist to do this.

Many patients will complete the reviews on the spot, especially if you have a tablet in the office already on the Google page. Others may do it while they're in their car returning home.

If you're having trouble with patients leaving a review, you can also offer an incentive such as a raffle entry, gift card, or promotional pricing.

We can't overstate how important it is to have online reviews. Your patients will often look up your reviews before they ever book an appointment with you.

A Well-Performing Website

What are the components of a well-performing website?

1. Ability to schedule directly on the website
2. Mobile optimization
3. Reduced waitlists—appointment availability

Appointment Scheduling Directly on Website

If you only implement one piece of advice in this entire book, it's this one: your practice website should directly include the *ability to schedule appointments*.

If your patients must call you to schedule an appointment, they will not do so as often as you'd like.

Millennials and Generation Z do not prefer to talk on the phone. They want to be able to schedule online quickly and easily.

Mobile Optimization

Mobile optimization means that your website should be easy to navigate on a smartphone. If you dig into your Google analytics on your webpage, it will clearly tell you how much of your traffic is mobile versus desktop versus tablet. If you're unfamiliar with Google Analytics, please do research on it immediately. It will show you a full breakdown of your traffic sourced from Google.

One the next page is a snippet of what you'll see in Google Analytics.

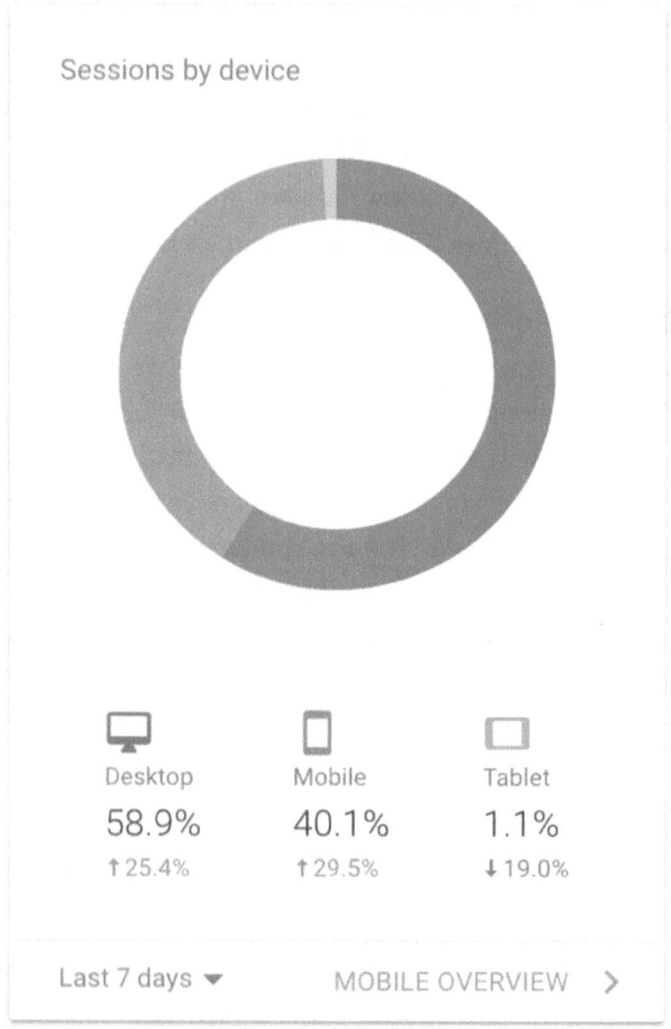

©2018 Google LLC, used with permission. Google and the Google logo are registered trademarks of Google LLC.

    This example highlights the type of traffic for this website over the past seven days. 58.9% of the traffic was from a desktop, 40.1% was from a phone, and 1.1% was from a tablet.

    In the example, if the site described in the image above did not optimize for mobile users, 40.1% of the website traffic would have a diminished experience.

For some reason, in our experience, many providers opt for a very low-cost firm or freelancer to build their websites. Some even choose to do it themselves.

We don't recommend this route. We cannot recommend not skimping here enough. Instead, hire a reputable designer or a firm. It doesn't need to cost thousands of dollars, but it shouldn't be a few bucks either.

The reasons for this are numerous.

1. When corners are cut, mobile interface quality is the first to go.
2. Many sites need to be optimized for speed and need to include a scheduling tool. Site speed also tends to suffer with lower cost options because increasing site speed can be quite technical and time-consuming. In addition, a private practice website without the ability to schedule appointments online might as well not exist.
3. Your site will be updated several times, which means you want fast communication with your website developer. Some places will respond within twenty-four hours, and others may take up to a week. Can you imagine the lost revenue if your site were down and you didn't have a response within a week from your developer?
4. SEO standards change often. In the world of website development, you get what you pay for.
5. You will be uploading blog posts onto your site, so you need a backend interface for this feature.

If for some reason you're still eager to do this on your own, we recommend building your site using Squarespace or Wix. Both sites have great templates that are easy to use, and both offer the proper infrastructure for SEO. They also have drag-and-drop designs to help you avoid dealing with pesky coding or many of the technical aspects.

Reduce Your Waitlist

Your goal is to decrease your waitlist to under one week. If patients have to wait a month to see you, you're going to lose a ton of business. Generally, patients want to be seen as quickly as possible.

Most people would prefer to schedule their appointment through a website and be seen within three to four days.

If your clinic is busy and you just don't have any time for new appointments for a full month, you may want to start hiring another provider, because you are not capitalizing on your revenue potential.

If feasible for your practice, try to leave time in your day for same-day appointments. This helps to offset cancellations and allows for walk-ins. Sometimes patients won't wait three days for an appointment and will just shop around for another provider. We would recommend two or three slots for same-day appointments or more with additional providers onboard.

Conclusion on Millennials

Marketing to millennials is not rocket science.

Millennials are your new patients, so please communicate with them in the way they communicate. To do so, we just need to make sure we're doing three major things:

1. Be present on social media
2. Have online reviews of your clinic available
3. Have a very professional website where patients can easily schedule online appointments

CHAPTER 11

Now, Take Action

"Freedom, financial independence and impact on an even greater scale are all very possible to achieve by taking action on the content you've read."

Information alone does not allow us to achieve our goals; otherwise, we would all be billionaires with six-pack abs. Instead, it is the intentional implementation of proven strategies and tactics backed by consistency that gets results.

Take Action

Practice owners need to think of themselves as business owners and implement the proven marketing strategies discussed in this book that will help them grow and thrive in any market condition.

Working smarter requires leveraging the tools, strategies, and tactics covered in this book. We've come across many private practice owners who are earning in the high six or near seven figures annually but need to work until the late hours every evening.

That's not a life.

If creating a larger practice or having a better quality of life appeals to you, give the strategies outlined in this book a shot.

You will notice a significant change in two areas: (1) income will increase, and (2) time commitment at work will decrease. We wrote this book to help high-quality practices excel at reaching more patients while reducing time and resources needed for marketing.

What to do Next

To help you get started, here are some actionable instructions to begin your marketing efforts. We wanted to revisit a checklist of items we introduced in Chapter 1. By now, a lot of these items should make much more sense to help you take the next steps in exponentially growing your practice.

In summary, below is a review of the "Jumpstart Checklist" found in Chapter 1:

- Create a unique selling proposition (USP)
- Integrate the USP across all of your marketing and communications
- Re-engage with your patient base via email
- Explore strategic alliances to expand your referral network
- Leverage digital marketing with targeted search to attract your ideal patient
- Understand and monitor the "Three Essential Avenues for Revenue Growth"
- Optimize your patient's experience by following the formula in Chapter 4
- Make it easy for patients to find you online and schedule an appointment
- Implement the step-by-step marketing automation found in Chapter 5
- Easily create content and distribute two to three times per week; outsource if necessary
- Implement the "Top 5 Ways to 'WOW' Your Patients" to improve patient loyalty and increase repeat business
- Consider the benefits of outsourcing, which includes hiring a virtual assistant at low-cost to help free up your time to serve more patients
- Leverage the recommendations in Chapter 9 to improve how easily prospective patients can find your practice online through search engines such as Google

- If millennials are a vital component of the patient base you serve or want to serve, implement the marketing strategies found in our chapter dedicated to "Marketing to Millennials"
- BONUS: Consider the benefits of precepting as a method to "test drive" future employees, participate in training future providers, and increase the revenue to your practice

Based on our experience working with private practices, we genuinely know that the above checklist can dramatically benefit the performance of your practice if you implement one item at a time. Marketing can become overwhelming and expensive if not approached in a systematic method.

Our hope is that now you are armed with the knowledge and tools necessary to take your practice to the next level!

To your success!

BONUS CHAPTER 12

Why Every Practice Should Consider Precepting

"If you currently own a private practice with four different providers and you don't precept students, you are losing out on $24,000-$40,000 in additional income every year."

This chapter didn't fit within the scope of this book and was moved at the last round of editing. However, we both agreed that the topic of this chapter needed to be written as it relates to dramatically increasing your practice revenue.

What is a Preceptor and Precepting?

In short, a preceptor is an experienced practitioner who provides supervision during clinical practice and facilitates the application of theory to practice for nursing graduate students.

Currently, precepting is an excellent revenue source a lot of practices are not taking advantage of. In many cases, providers are unaware they can receive compensation by precepting students.

Many times, providers ask:

> "Can precepting REALLY add revenue to my practice?"

There's a misconception where many practice owners believe precepting is only a hindrance and compensation is too low to justify the added responsibility.

Many preceptors earn an average of an additional $6,000–$10,000 in their clinics per provider per year, and compensation is typically provided per student and delivered within two weeks of a student starting their rotation.

This means that preceptors receive full compensation before the student finishes their placement, which is a boost to cash acceleration for the practice.

In graduate nursing education, there's a massive demand for qualified nurse practitioner preceptors. Every semester, thousands of prospective APRNs are delaying graduation because of the inability to locate clinical sites. Precepting graduate nursing students will not only add an additional income source, but you'll also be able to assist an APRN in graduating!

What Are the Benefits of Precepting?

Additional Revenue

Diversifying income streams is critical for any business, especially in healthcare, as revenue cycle timelines can vary and delay your cash flow. From a per patient revenue standpoint, being a provider can be quite lucrative, as we saw above. However, this revenue is largely determined by the number of patients seen by the student.

With the tools and resources in this book, you are now armed to grow your patient base as rapidly as you choose, and thereby capitalize on the additional revenue sources available with precepting.

Another Benefit of Precepting - "Test Driving" Graduates to Hire

Many preceptors who have the goal of expanding their practice find it invaluable to precept, as it basically allows for the chance to interview candidates as they serve your practice and you collect revenue for teaching them.

Healthcare students, especially NPs and PAs, are ready to practice immediately after graduation. For many preceptors, if you have a student who is in their last semester of their program, the timing is right for you to determine if you'd like to extend them an offer for full-time employment.

As a preceptor, you'll have the time (typically six to eight weeks) to evaluate the skills of the students, including their attitude and aptitude during the designated clinical rotation. It's *not* uncommon to see preceptors extend full-time positions to students once they graduate.

As a preceptor, you'll have access to highly talented students before they are recruited in the open market, therefore avoiding a bidding war for hiring. The benefit to the students, of course, is having a position waiting for them upon graduation.

Utilizing the duration of the clinical placement is a great way to determine cultural fit as well —something especially critical for small team environments, where one additional person can really impact the synergy of team productivity.

A Common Objection to Precepting is Time Constraints

Some potential preceptors reading this right now might be thinking, "Oh my God, I want to teach, but I just don't have the time"

It's a completely valid thought, but many providers have been able to address the time commitment issue by utilizing the following strategies:

1. Spread the teaching responsibility to other members of the clinic: If you have multiple providers in the clinic, the teaching time can be spread out amongst the staff.
2. Set charting expectations: Charting responsibilities can fall on the NP student to complete outside of clinic hours.
3. Choose the best schedule for your clinic: Vary the days and times students come to the clinic. Choose the schedule that best ensures your clinic is least impacted.
4. Allow students to "tag-team." Check with the student's university, but most schools are comfortable with two students "tag-teaming" patients and providing treatment plans as a team with the experienced practitioner.

In conclusion, precepting has many benefits to Advanced Practice Providers who have their own clinic. It can be a great way to boost income as well as "test drive" potential new hires, as the practice continues to grow. If the marketing principles in this book are coupled with the choice to become a preceptor, practice revenue can really take off as you begin to expand your impact on the health of your local community.

ABOUT THE AUTHORS

KRISH CHOPRA is the CEO & Co-Founder of NPHub. His mission is to empower underserved communities and is currently focused on helping Nurse Practitioners become successful entrepreneurs. His belief is simple: Nurse Practitioners are the future of primary care in the United States.

In 2019, Krish was selected in Inc.'s 30 under 30 list, a prestigious recognition for rising stars in entrepreneurship. Recognized by Medium as a Top Writer in Leadership in 2018, he regularly contributes to major publications such as Forbes, Fast Company, Thrive Global, Huffington Post, and Inc.

Krish Chopra is a graduate of the University of Michigan and is also a member of the YEC, an invite-only group comprised of the world's most successful entrepreneurs aged 45 and younger.

NAMAR AL-GANAS, MHA is a successful management consultant with over fifteen years of experience in the healthcare industry. His mission is to positively impact the financial health of providers, so they can take the best care of their patients in the communities they serve across the United States.

Throughout his career, Namar has led the successful completion of high-impact engagements for over 100 hospitals and physician practices across the country, resulting in greater revenue performance and improved business operations.

As a native of St. Paul, MN, he is a graduate of the Carlson School of Management at the University of Minnesota. He received his graduate degree in health administration from Cornell University. He is passionate about lifelong learning, wellness, staying active, and enjoys spending time with his fiancé and friends. Namar lives in Atlanta, GA.